The Samsung Galaxy S24 Guide

Elevate Your Smartphone Game With Samsung's Finest, Your Complete Handbook For The Best Smartphone Experience

Callista Christopher

Table of Contents

6

Introduction

Overview of Samsung's Galaxy S24 Series

The Samsung Galaxy S24 Series represents a new apex in the growth of mobile technology, combining innovation, intelligence, and elegance seamlessly. As the follow-up to the renowned S23 Series, the S24 Series pushes the boundaries of what is possible, changing the smartphone experience for people worldwide.

The Significance of Galaxy AI in the Mobile Experience

At the core of the Galaxy S24 Series lies the innovative Galaxy AI, a powerful artificial intelligence engine that elevates daily experiences to new heights.

Galaxy AI is more than simply a feature; it's an essential component of the device's DNA, improving functionality, convenience, and user engagement in ways never before seen.

The incorporation of AI into the mobile experience demonstrates Samsung's dedication to making technology more intuitive and user-centered. Galaxy AI turns the smartphone into a proactive companion by learning user behavior, preferences, and context, anticipating requirements and giving tailored answers.

To set the tone for the S24 Series exploration, TM Roh, President and Head of Mobile eXperience Business at Samsung Electronics, highlights the company's ambition and commitment to providing cutting-edge technology. Roh's statements encapsulate the core of Samsung's mission: to revolutionize the mobile experience and deliver people with a device that exceeds expectations.

In a recent press release, TM Roh stated that "The Galaxy S24 Series represents a quantum leap in smartphone innovation." With the power of Galaxy AI, we're bringing a new way to connect with technology, not simply a new phone. It's all about empowering people, transforming search, unleashing creativity, and providing the most intelligent experience ever.

The S24 Series exemplifies Samsung's constant pursuit of perfection, and we're delighted to see how it improves our consumers' lives."

Galaxy AI Features Overview

Galaxy AI is the brains behind the Galaxy S24 Series, bringing a slew of features aimed at simplifying, improving, and personalizing the user experience.

Galaxy AI effortlessly integrates into different elements of the smartphone, including intelligent assistants and powerful search capabilities, making it a genuine companion for consumers in their daily life.

One of Galaxy AI's distinguishing advantages is its ability to enhance ordinary encounters. The S24 Series offers Live Translate, which eliminates language barriers with real-time translation capabilities.

Whether you're chatting with friends, coworkers, or strangers, Live Translate guarantees that language barriers don't impede productive communication.

This capability is extended to Interpreter, which provides real-time transcription of conversations, making it an important tool for business meetings, interviews, and other situations.

Another notable feature of Galaxy AI is its ability to refine conversational tones via Chat Assist. This section examines text messages, emails, and other kinds of digital communication and recommends ways to improve the tone and intelligibility of the communications.

It's like having a personal writing coach built into your smartphone, ensuring that your words are understood and communicate the right emotions.

Beyond conversation, Galaxy AI transforms online search with Circle to Search, a tool created in conjunction with Google. This gesture-driven search feature allows users to draw a circle on their screen, which triggers a search for the information within the circle. It's a visually appealing and effective approach to locate information that eliminates the need for typical text-based inquiries.

In the next sections of this chapter, we will go deeper into each of these features, looking at how they reinvent the user experience and set the Galaxy S24 Series apart in the competitive smartphone landscape. From boosting communication to transforming search, Galaxy AI is the driving force behind the intelligence built in all of these extraordinary technologies.

Encouraging Everyday Experiences

In today's fast-paced, linked world, the Samsung Galaxy S24 Series, driven by Galaxy AI, is more than a smartphone; it's a companion that enhances everyday experiences.
Galaxy AI improves how consumers interact, organize, and manage their life by offering a spectrum of unique capabilities. In this part, we'll look at the Galaxy AI capabilities that aim to make every interaction smooth, intelligent, and barrier-free.

Galaxy AI Features Overview

Before we get into particular features, let's take a time to appreciate Galaxy AI's comprehensive approach. It is not enough to introduce discrete features; rather, it is necessary to create an ecosystem in which intelligence is seamlessly integrated into the fabric of the user experience.

The Galaxy AI Features Overview showcases the intelligence built into the S24 Series, demonstrating how it goes beyond the traditional bounds of smartphone capabilities. From improving communication to improving organization, Galaxy AI transforms the smartphone into a flexible tool that responds to the user's demands.

Live Translation for Barrier-free Communication

Communication is at the heart of human contact, and Live Translate is Galaxy AI's solution for breaking down language boundaries. Whether you're traveling, working with foreign colleagues, or interacting with friends from various linguistic backgrounds, Live Translate makes sure that language barriers don't impede productive communication.

This function supports a wide range of languages, allowing users to receive real-time translations of both text and speech. Imagine being in a different location and effortlessly speaking with natives, or attending a worldwide business conference without the need for a specialized translation. Live Translate makes these possibilities a reality, building a global society in which language is no longer a barrier but rather a bridge that connects people from all over the world.

Furthermore, Live Translate interacts smoothly with messaging apps, allowing users to engage in multilingual discussions without switching programs. It demonstrates Samsung's commitment to building a connected world where communication is inclusive and accessible to everyone.

An interpreter for real-time conversation transcription

Building on the foundation of Live Translate, the S24 Series offers Interpreter, a function that elevates communication by offering real-time transcription of conversations. Whether it's a business meeting, an interview, or a casual talk, Interpreter converts every spoken word into text, resulting in a useful record for future reference.

Interpreting is more than just transcribing; it is about increasing accessibility and diversity. Users with hearing impairments can benefit from text-based representations of spoken words, which prevents them from missing out on important information or experiences. This is consistent with Samsung's commitment to using technology for the greater good, ensuring that advancements are not just cutting-edge, but also contribute to a more inclusive society.

In addition to transcribing, Interpreter allows users to search inside the transcribed text, making it easier to find information quickly. This functionality is especially beneficial in corporate settings, where obtaining certain data from a lengthy meeting discussion is simple.

Chat Assist to Perfect Conversational Tone

Effective communication involves effectively transmitting emotions, intentions, and tones, in addition to language. Chat Assist is a Galaxy AI function that acts as your own writing coach, evaluating text messages, emails, and other forms of digital communication and making suggestions to improve tone and clarity.

How many times have you sent a message and wished you had phrased yourself differently? Chat Assist is available to guarantee that your communications are understood and express the desired sentiments.

It accomplishes this by understanding the context of your communications and providing modest suggestions to improve your tone, making your communication more effective and empathic.

Chat Assist works in the background, learning from your conversation habits and tailoring its suggestions to your individual style. It's like having an intelligent friend that leads you to more meaningful and nuanced conversation, thereby deepening your relationships with others.

Android Auto Integration for Secure In-Car Communication

In a day where multitasking is the norm, the addition of Android Auto to the Galaxy S24 Series elevates in-car communication to a new level of safety and convenience. Whether you're commuting to work or taking a road trip, being connected without compromising safety is critical.

Android Auto Integration enables customers to access key functionalities of their Galaxy S24 Series while keeping their eyes on the road. The integration allows users to stay connected while driving, whether they are making calls, sending messages, or receiving directions.

Voice commands are crucial to this integration, allowing consumers to operate their devices with natural language. Whether dictating texts, making calls, or asking for directions, hands-free capability improves safety while allowing users to maintain control of their devices.

Furthermore, Android Auto works smoothly with navigation applications, offering real-time updates and instructions right on the car's display. This not only simplifies the navigation experience, but also lowers distractions, resulting in a safer driving environment.

Note and Transcript Assist for Enhanced Organization

Staying organized in the midst of daily life can be difficult for many people. Note Assist and Transcript Assist are Galaxy AI technologies that ease organization, allowing users to easily manage their notes, documents, and critical information.

Note Assist is a smart note-taking companion that goes beyond standard note applications.
It detects important information in your notes, such as dates, places, and tasks, and makes appropriate suggestions.
For example, if you write down a meeting time, Note Assist may offer you to make a reminder or add an item to your calendar.

Transcript Assist, on the other hand, changes the way you manage transcripts and crucial papers. Transcript Assist uses extensive language processing skills to summarize long papers, highlight significant aspects, and even produce actionable insights.
This is especially useful for professionals who work with large reports, interviews, or research materials since it dramatically decreases the time and effort necessary to extract important information.

Both Note Assist and Transcript Assist work well with other productivity tools, resulting in a unified environment that improves everyday job efficiency.

Whether you're a student, a professional, or someone who runs a busy family, these features are intended to serve as virtual assistants, ensuring that you keep organized and on top of your obligations.

To summarize, the Galaxy S24 Series, with its suite of Galaxy AI capabilities, is more than simply a smartphone; it's a revolutionary tool that improves everyday encounters. From breaking down language barriers to honing conversational tones, assuring safe in-car communication, and improving organization, Galaxy AI is building a smarter, more connected world. As we progress through the chapters of this guidebook, we will look at the various ways in which the S24 Series redefines what is possible in the world of mobile technology.

Revolutionizing Internet Search

In the ever-changing environment of digital technology, the Samsung Galaxy S24 Series includes ground-breaking capabilities intended at redefining how people engage with internet searches.

Circle to Search with Google, Gesture-Driven Search, Generative AI-Powered Overviews, and Location-Based Search Enhancements—these innovations transform the search experience by making it more intuitive, customized, and efficient.

In this chapter, we'll look at how these elements work together to revolutionize the landscape of online search, providing consumers with a smooth and intelligent experience in the digital arena.

Introduction to Circle: Search using Google

Imagine a future in which looking for information is as simple as drawing a circle on your screen. Google's Circle to Search tool brings this concept to life.

It is more than simply a search bar or a voice command; it is a natural motion that effortlessly connects the physical and digital worlds.

Circle to Search allows users to start a search by drawing a circle on their device's screen. The circle functions as a dynamic search portal, quickly activating Google's search capabilities. Whether you're reading an article, exploring social media, or viewing photographs, the circle serves as a direct access to a plethora of information.

This novel technique to search demonstrates Samsung's dedication to streamlining user interactions.
Circle to Search eliminates the need to switch applications or write searches, providing a smooth and natural approach to navigate the digital universe.
It demonstrates how technology can adapt to human behavior, making the search experience both efficient and pleasant.

How Does Gesture-Driven Search Work

Gesture-Driven Search enhances user involvement by using intuitive motions to browse and improve search results.

In an age where touchscreens are the standard, Gesture-Driven Search adds a level of complexity by allowing users to engage with their devices in a more tactile and expressive manner.

Swipe gestures, pinch-to-zoom, and other natural hand movements become the language with which people interact with their smartphones. When looking for photographs, for example, a single swipe allows visitors to easily navigate through results. Pinch-to-zoom actions allow for a deeper investigation of details, giving users a tactile sensation similar to turning through magazine pages.

The beauty of Gesture-Driven Search is its flexibility to accommodate to individual preferences. Users may tailor gestures to their preferences and use habits, resulting in a customized and fluid search experience.

Whether you're a casual user or a power searcher, Gesture-Driven Search adjusts to your individual preferences, making the search process not only quick but also pleasurable.

Furthermore, Gesture-Driven Search goes beyond the scope of search engines. It connects easily with other programs, allowing users to navigate numerous features using gestures. This comprehensive integration guarantees that the search experience is not restricted to a single context, but rather becomes an integrated component of the whole user interface.

Generative AI-powered overviews for specific searches

Finding relevant and clear information fast is difficult in this day and age of information overload.

Generative AI-Powered Overviews solve this issue by summarizing key insights for specific queries.

Consider running a difficult research query and obtaining a simplified summary that emphasizes important points and vital facts.

This feature goes beyond standard search results by using powerful generative AI algorithms to evaluate and summarize information. Whether you're researching a topic for work, studying for a test, or simply exploring your hobbies, Generative AI-Powered Overviews make the process easier by delivering concise information at a glance.

For example, if you're looking for information about a historical event, the overview may include crucial dates, major individuals, and the overall context. This saves time while also ensuring that consumers receive the most relevant information without having to trawl through lengthy articles or documents.

Generative AI-powered Overviews demonstrate Samsung's dedication to harnessing AI for the benefit of users. It's more than simply offering search results; it's about providing insights that allow users to make educated decisions and have a deeper grasp of the topics they research.

Location-Based Search Enhancements

One of the most essential characteristics of human exploration is the relationship between people and places. Location-depending Search Enhancements identify the value of context in search queries and provide a more personalized and relevant search experience depending on the user's location.

Imagine going down a street and wondering about neighboring eateries, historical sites, or activities.
With Location-Based search enhancements, the Galaxy S24 Series recognizes your context and returns search results that are spatially appropriate. This goes beyond mere proximity-based suggestions; it's about knowing the user's surroundings and offering information to improve their real-world experience.

For example, if you're visiting a new city, a location-based search can offer you not only surrounding attractions but also information on local customs, events, and famous restaurants. This tool is a game changer for travelers, adventurers, and anybody looking to interact with their environment in a deeper way.

Furthermore, location-based search enhancements apply to everyday chores. Need to locate the local gas station, pharmacy, or grocery store? The Galaxy S24 Series anticipates your requirements and ensures that search results are relevant to your present location, making it a useful companion for navigating both familiar and unexpected territory.

The Impact on Discovering Information

At its root, the revolution in internet search is about more than just making the process faster and more convenient.
It is about turning the act of searching into a voyage of discovery. The combination of Circle to Search, Gesture-Driven Search, Generative AI-Powered Overviews, and Location-Based Search Enhancements offers an ecosystem that allows users to navigate the enormous digital environment with intelligence and convenience.

Discovering information becomes an immersive experience, with search features tailored to user behavior, preferences, and context. Whether you're an inquisitive student, a professional researcher, or seeking local suggestions, the Galaxy S24 Series allows you to access information in a way that meets your own requirements and interests.

As we progress through the chapters of this handbook, the topic of intelligent exploration will become clearer. The innovative search functions of the Galaxy S24 Series represent a fundamental shift in how we interact with the digital world, paving the way for a future in which technology blends effortlessly with human curiosity, creativity, and the intrinsic urge to explore and discover.

Unleash Creativity with ProVisual Engine

The Samsung Galaxy S24 Series advances smartphone photography significantly with its ProVisual Engine, a cutting-edge package of capabilities meant to unleash users' full creative potential.

The ProVisual Engine, with its unrivaled zoom capabilities and new AI-powered editing tools, is ready to transform how we capture and improve visual moments. In this chapter, we look at the numerous aspects of the ProVisual Engine, including how it enables users to unleash their creativity and capture the world in unique ways.

Overview of the ProVisual Engine

At the core of the Galaxy S24 Series' photographic expertise is the ProVisual Engine, a sophisticated system that combines hardware and software improvements to give a truly remarkable visual experience.

The ProVisual Engine is more than just a collection of features; it's a unified and intelligent platform that ensures every shot and video captures the spirit of the moment.

The engine blends superior camera technology with AI-powered algorithms, resulting in a synergy that improves image quality, clarity, and visual appeal.
Whether you're a skilled photographer or a casual hobbyist, the ProVisual Engine adjusts to your skill level, boosting your photography game and turning every snap into a masterpiece.

Quad Tele System and Improved Zoom Capability

Zoom capabilities are frequently a distinguishing feature in smartphone photography, and the Galaxy S24 Series sets new benchmarks with its Quad Tele System.
This technique, which consists of numerous telephoto lenses functioning in tandem, enables users to easily move between optical zoom levels, capturing distant scenes with unparalleled clarity.

Imagine attending a performance and effortlessly zooming in to capture the performer's nuanced emotions, or going outside and bringing distant vistas into clear focus. The Quad Tele System preserves every detail, allowing users to explore and position their images without losing image quality.

Enhanced Zoom Capabilities go beyond hardware and include AI-driven innovations that automatically optimize digital zoom. The ProVisual Engine analyzes the environment in real time, modifying settings to guarantee that digitally zoomed photos retain sharpness and detail. This combination of hardware and software results in a zoom experience that is both strong and amazingly sophisticated.

Nightography: Improved Low-Light Photography

Nightography, a novel feature inside the ProVisual Engine, makes shooting moments in low-light circumstances even more appealing.

Recognizing that some of life's most unforgettable events take place in the dim light of twilight or under the stars, nightography elevates low-light photography to the level of art.

Nightography, which uses powerful low-light sensors and AI algorithms, improves the camera's sensitivity to light, allowing users to capture images with stunning clarity and minimum noise.

Whether it's a metropolis bathed in the soothing glow of streetlights or a candid moment by candlelight, nightography guarantees that low-light situations no longer limit the ability to create breathtaking graphics.

The ProVisual Engine's Nightography function does more than simply capture what the eyes perceive; it also preserves the mood and ambiance of the occasion. Users can create deeper visual tales with better low-light photography, which captures the ambiance and emotions that accompany situations after sunset.

AI Editing Tools: Erase, Re-compose, and Remaster

The ProVisual Engine's creative powers extend beyond photo capture, with the introduction of a suite of AI-powered editing tools that revolutionize post-production possibilities. These tools include Erase, Re-compose, and Remaster, each with their own set of functions for enhancing and customizing photos.

Erase: Have you ever caught the ideal moment only to discover an undesirable item in the frame? Erase simply resolves this issue.

Erase uses powerful AI algorithms to accurately detect and eliminate undesired components from images, completely merging the backdrop to create a pure image.

Whether it's a photobomber in a gorgeous landscape or an unintended item in a picture, Erase keeps your images focused on their intended topic.

Re-compose: Composition is an important component of photography, and Re-compose allows users to tweak and improve their compositions after the shot has been taken. This AI tool examines the items in the frame and makes recommendations for cropping or altering the composition to provide a more visually attractive outcome.

It's like having a virtual photographic assistant guide you to the ideal composition.

Remaster: Remaster brings your images to a new degree of visual brilliance. This AI-powered tool improves image quality by assessing and adjusting characteristics like sharpness, color balance, and dynamic range.

Whether you're editing a photo taken in difficult lighting settings or want to add a pop of brightness to your images, Remaster guarantees that they stand out with remarkable clarity and detail.

These AI editing tools mark a fundamental shift in how consumers approach post-processing. The ProVisual Engine does more than just record events; it allows users to develop and polish their visual storytelling, guaranteeing that each photograph matches their creative vision.

Edit Suggestion and Generative Editing Features

Recognizing that not every user is an experienced picture editor, the ProVisual Engine includes editing suggestions and generative editing features.

These sophisticated features use AI to evaluate your photographs and make automatic suggestions for improvements, making the editing process more accessible to everyone.

Edit Suggestion: Consider taking a shot and, before you even start editing, the ProVisual Engine recommends upgrades based on the content and composition.

Edit Suggestion takes the uncertainty out of editing by providing unique ideas that match your style.

From correcting exposure to improving colors, these ideas are specific to each photo, ensuring that the editing process is not only efficient but also personalized to your photographs' distinct features.

Generative Editing Features: For those who prefer playing with creative alterations, the Generative Edit Features provide a plethora of options. These tools use generative AI algorithms to analyze your photographs and make creative edit suggestions that go beyond traditional upgrades.

The Generative Edit Features encourage users to experiment with new forms of visual expression, whether it's via the use of creative filters, dynamic collages, or innovative color grading techniques.

Edit Suggestion and Generative Edit Features work together to democratize the editing process, allowing users of all skill levels to access sophisticated advancements. The ProVisual Engine promotes unrestricted creativity by encouraging users to experiment, express, and reinterpret their visual storytelling.

Super HDR for lifelike previews

HDR (High Dynamic Spectrum) technology has become a photographic industry standard, allowing users to capture a wider spectrum of tones and details in tough lighting settings. The Galaxy S24 Series goes a step further with Super HDR, a function that not only improves the final image but also offers lifelike previews in real time.

When composing a photo, Super HDR analyzes the scene and dynamically adjusts exposure settings to imitate the final image's appearance. This real-time display allows users to record scenes with confidence, knowing exactly how the lighting conditions will affect the results.
Whether it's a backlit landscape or a portrait in bright sunshine, Super HDR allows users to make educated selections during the shooting process.

The lifelike previews provided by Super HDR provide for a more intuitive and engaging photographic experience. Users no longer have to rely exclusively on post-processing to produce the best results; the ProVisual Engine delivers a preview of the final product, allowing for creative tweaks at the point of recording.

Finally, the ProVisual Engine is more than simply a photo capture tool; it is the beginning of a new era of visual storytelling. From unmatched zoom capabilities and low-light photography advancements to AI-powered editing tools and lifelike HDR previews.

The Galaxy's Most Intelligent Experience Ever

The Samsung Galaxy S24 Series marks a new age in smartphone technology, providing the most intelligent and immersive experience yet. This chapter delves into the intelligence built into every component of the Galaxy S24 Series, which includes cutting-edge technologies and advancements in areas ranging from performance and displays to durability and design.

Enhanced Performance with the Snapdragon 8 Gen 3 Mobile Platform

The strong Snapdragon 8 Gen 3 Mobile Platform serves as the foundation for the Galaxy S24 Series' intelligence. Qualcomm's newest generation offers a significant advancement in mobile processing, providing unprecedented performance and efficiency.

Whether you're multitasking between resource-intensive apps or pushing the limits of mobile creativity, the Snapdragon 8 Gen 3 delivers a smooth and responsive experience.

The Galaxy S24 Series uses the platform's superior CPU, GPU, and AI capabilities to challenge consumer expectations. From speedier app launches to better graphics rendering, each encounter with the smartphone demonstrates the raw power and intelligence behind the hood. The Snapdragon 8 Gen 3 not only meets current needs but also future-proofs the Galaxy S24 Series, keeping it at the forefront of mobile performance for years to come.

Adaptive Refresh Rates to Improve Efficiency

Building on the foundation of improved performance is the clever use of variable refresh rates.

The Galaxy S24 Series has dynamic display technology, which adjusts the refresh rate in real time according to the material being viewed.

This not only provides a buttery-smooth experience during high-motion activities such as gaming, but it also saves battery life by reducing the refresh rate for static or less demanding material.

Imagine reading your social media feed at a low refresh rate in order to conserve power, then suddenly switching to a high refresh rate while playing a graphics-intensive game. This adaptive method maximizes the user experience by providing the best of both worlds: responsiveness and efficiency.

The Galaxy S24 Series automatically adjusts to your usage habits, giving you display performance that is both smart and spectacular.

Game Capabilities and Ray Tracing

For dedicated gamers, the Galaxy S24 Series elevates mobile gaming to a new level of immersion.

With its gaming-focused features and the Snapdragon 8 Gen 3's graphical capability, this series increases the standard for mobile gaming performance.

Ray tracing, a technology formerly reserved for high-end gaming PCs and consoles, now puts cinematic-quality visuals in your hands.

Ray tracing mimics light's interaction with virtual objects, resulting in realistic shadows, reflections, and lighting effects. Whether you're exploring enormous virtual worlds or competing in fast-paced online fights, ray tracing improves game visual fidelity, making each moment more exciting. The Galaxy S24 Series doesn't just play games; it takes them to the next level of realism and excitement.

Vibrant Displays and Vision Booster

The Galaxy S24 Series' intelligence extends to its brilliant screens, which include Vision Booster technology.

Vision Booster goes beyond standard display upgrades by using AI algorithms to dynamically alter contrast, color temperature, and brightness based on environmental illumination and the material being seen.

This adaptive method guarantees that the display stays brilliant and legible in any lighting, whether in direct sunshine or in a poorly lit room. Vision Booster not only improves visual clarity, but it also minimizes eye strain by tailoring the display characteristics to the surrounding conditions. The Galaxy S24 Series is more than simply a smartphone; it's a visual companion that intelligently adjusts to your viewing habits and the world around you.

Using Corning Gorilla Armor for Durability

In pursuit of an intelligent and sturdy smartphone, the Galaxy S24 Series incorporates Corning Gorilla Armor, demonstrating a dedication to durability without sacrificing design. The Galaxy S24 Series' creative use of sophisticated materials guarantees that it can survive the rigors of daily living, including resistance to drops, scratches, and impacts.

Corning Gorilla Armor is more than simply a protective layer; it's a barrier that keeps the device's elegant design and visual appeal intact. The Galaxy S24 Series' clever blend of robustness and elegance guarantees that it not only works well but also looks good, distinguishing itself as a sturdy and stylish companion in your palm.

Design enhancements and screen sizes

A variety of design upgrades round off the clever package, elevating the Galaxy S24 variety to new heights of elegance. The meticulously created design language perfectly merges form and function, resulting in a gadget that not only works well but also feels luxurious in your hand.

The Galaxy S24 Series has a variety of screen sizes to accommodate a wide range of user tastes, from those who value compactness to those who want large screens. The intelligent design extends to button placement, tactile feel, and general ergonomics, resulting in a device that is both pleasant to handle and enjoyable to use.

Advanced Security and Privacy

In an age where digital connectedness is the foundation of our everyday lives, protecting the security and privacy of personal data has never been more important.

The Samsung Galaxy S24 Series makes a significant step forward in this area, with a sophisticated suite of security features and privacy settings that establish new standards for mobile device safety.

An Overview of Samsung Knox

The Galaxy S24 Series' security architecture is built around Samsung Knox, a robust and multi-layered security platform. Knox is more than simple security software; it is a whole ecosystem intended to safeguard the device from the ground up. From hardware to software, Knox creates a secure foundation that protects against a wide range of threats.

Knox's secure boot procedure guarantees that the device starts up securely, preventing unwanted changes to the operating system. Real-time kernel protection, which guards against kernel-level attacks, is an addition to this fundamental security feature. The combination of secure boot and kernel protection provides a strong barrier against malicious software that seeks to undermine the device's integrity.

Furthermore, Samsung Knox's protective umbrella is extended to the application layer using containerization technology. This feature provides a secure and isolated workplace, also known as the Knox workplace, where important apps and data may be stored. Even if the device is hacked, the secure container protects sensitive information from unwanted access.

In addition to safeguarding the device, Samsung Knox enables secure connections with the larger digital environment. Knox's Secure Folder function lets users set up a private, encrypted place on their device. An additional layer of authentication protects this area, which is completely different from the typical user experience and acts as a safe vault for private conversations, programs, and information.

User Control and Advanced Intelligence Settings

Recognizing that customers' security preferences vary, the Galaxy S24 Series has enhanced intelligence settings that provide users with greater control over their device's security and privacy choices. These settings use AI insights to deliver tailored suggestions and adaptive security measures.

For example, the device may learn user behavior patterns and recommend the best security setups depending on individual usage. This might include suggestions on when to activate secure Wi-Fi connections, change app permissions, or do security assessments. By incorporating intelligence into decision-making, the Galaxy S24 Series guarantees that security measures are not only effective but also user-friendly and adapted to individual requirements.

An Introduction to Knox Matrix and Passkeys

The Galaxy S24 Series takes personalization and security to the next level with Knox Matrix and Passkeys.

Knox Matrix is an intelligent security matrix that adjusts dynamically to user behavior and device circumstances.

It continually assesses risk indicators and modifies security parameters accordingly.

Passkeys, used inside the Knox Matrix architecture, are a new solution to user authentication. Traditional passwords and PINs are frequently vulnerable to security breaches, either because of predictable patterns or flaws in the authentication process. Passkeys challenge this paradigm by proposing dynamic and context-aware authentication techniques.

Passkeys, for example, might include biometric data, contextual information (such as location and time), and user behavior patterns. This multidimensional approach not only improves security, but it also makes the authentication process easier for consumers to understand and utilize.

Enhanced Data Protection with Seven Years of Updates

The commitment to security goes beyond the initial purchase of the gadget. The Galaxy S24 Series provides seven years of frequent security upgrades, guaranteeing that customers are protected from evolving risks throughout the device's lifespan.

This industry-leading support demonstrates Samsung's commitment to long-term device security and user peace of mind.

Aside from software upgrades, the Galaxy S24 Series has enhanced data protection methods. End-to-end encryption protects communication channels against unlawful interception of sensitive information.

In addition, the device uses secure data storage techniques to ensure that user data is safeguarded at all times, whether at rest or in transit.

Biometric information, such as fingerprints and face recognition data, is also protected under the improved data protection standards.

These biometric credentials are safely saved in the device's Trusted Execution Environment (TEE), which is a secure enclave apart from the ordinary operating system. This isolation means that even in the unlikely case of a security breach, biometric data is protected.

Finally, the Galaxy S24 Series promotes user control and privacy while including cutting-edge security technologies. From Samsung Knox's strong foundation to enhanced intelligence settings, revolutionary Knox Matrix and Passkeys, and a commitment to seven years of upgrades, every piece of the security architecture is methodically engineered to deliver an unrivaled degree of protection. In a digital environment where dangers are continually developing, the Galaxy S24 Series serves as a beacon of confidence, providing consumers with a safe and private mobile experience that exceeds expectations.

The Next Steps in Samsung's Environmental Journey

In an era of rising environmental awareness and sustainability concerns, firms are increasingly accepting responsibility for their environmental effects.

Samsung, a global technological behemoth, is at the vanguard of this trend, with a pledge to advance its environmental efforts. The Galaxy S24 Series, Samsung's latest flagship device, marks a big step forward in the company's environmental journey.

This chapter digs into the main components that constitute the next stage of Samsung's environmental commitment.

Recycled Materials in the Galaxy S24 Series

The use of recycled materials in the manufacture of electrical equipment is a critical step in reducing their environmental impact. The Galaxy S24 Series illustrates Samsung's commitment to this philosophy by including a significant percentage of recycled materials into its manufacture.

From the exterior to the interior components, Samsung has carefully chosen recycled materials to produce a more sustainable and environmentally friendly gadget.

This goal is consistent with the rising global concern about the environmental effects of electronic waste. By using recycled materials, Samsung not only reduces the extraction of fresh resources but also helps to reduce the total environmental impact of smartphone manufacture.

Use of recycled cobalt and rare earth elements

The Galaxy S24 Series makes a special attempt to use recycled cobalt and rare earth metals in its construction. These materials, which are frequently derived from mined minerals, have long aroused ethical and environmental issues owing to mining methods and their influence on local ecosystems.

By using recycled cobalt and rare earth metals, Samsung takes a major step toward resolving these issues.

The utilization of recycled materials decreases the need for new mining activities while also encouraging responsible resource management. This step demonstrates Samsung's commitment to ethical sourcing and its role in promoting a circular economy.

Commitment to Extended Product Lifecycle

Samsung's environmental strategy includes promoting longer product lifecycles. The Galaxy S24 Series is built for durability and endurance, with the goal of extending the device's usable life beyond the regular update cycle. This strategy is consistent with the concepts of the circular economy, in which things are intended to endure longer, be readily repaired, and finally be recycled at the end of their existence.

Samsung encourages people to keep their devices for longer periods of time by offering software updates, repairability programs, and high build quality. This not only decreases total electrical waste, but it also lessens the environmental effect of new gadget development.

UL EcoLogo Certification and Carbon Footprint Verification

To give consumers transparent information about the Galaxy S24 Series' environmental effect, Samsung obtained third-party certifications and verifications.

The gadget has the coveted UL ECOLOGO Certification, which indicates that it passes stringent environmental performance requirements. This accreditation guarantees customers that the Galaxy S24 Series has passed rigorous testing to ensure it adheres to environmentally friendly standards.

Samsung has also undertaken carbon footprint certification for the Galaxy S24 Series. This procedure entails doing a thorough analysis of the greenhouse gas emissions associated with the device's full lifespan, from raw material extraction to production, shipping, usage, and disposal. The carbon footprint verification demonstrates Samsung's commitment to understanding and reducing the environmental effect of its products.

Samsung's Environmental Goals For 2025

Looking ahead, Samsung has set lofty environmental targets for 2025, laying the groundwork for future sustainability improvements. These objectives span a wide range of the company's activities, from product creation to supply chain management.

Some significant features of Samsung's environmental aims are:

1. **Zero trash to Landfill:** Samsung strives to redirect all trash generated in its manufacturing sites away from landfills while encouraging appropriate waste management practices.

2. **Renewable Energy Use:** The corporation intends to increase its usage of renewable energy in its manufacturing plants, therefore lowering its dependency on nonrenewable sources.

3. **Water Conservation:** Samsung aims to reduce water usage in its production processes by promoting appropriate water management practices.

4. **Circular Economy Initiatives:** The firm intends to actively support the circular economy by expanding the use of recycled materials in its products and encouraging recycling initiatives.

5. **Eco-Friendly Packaging:** Samsung wants to improve the sustainability of its product packaging by employing more environmentally friendly materials and lowering total packaging waste.

By laying out these objectives, Samsung not only displays its commitment to environmental stewardship, but also encourages examination and accountability from stakeholders and customers.
The ambitious scope of these aims indicates Samsung's recognition of the importance and urgency of tackling global environmental concerns.

Finally, the Galaxy S24 Series exemplifies Samsung's ever-changing environmental strategy. Samsung is defining the future of sustainable technology by using recycled materials, committing to longer product lifecycles, obtaining third-party certifications, and setting ambitious environmental targets.

As customers value eco-friendly practices, Samsung's proactive approach not only matches current expectations but also establishes a precedent for the industry, demonstrating that cutting-edge technology and environmental stewardship can coexist.

Precision Technology with Elegance in Every Detail

The Galaxy S24 Series, Samsung's latest flagship product, is the height of precision technology and elegance, with painstaking design aspects that set new benchmarks for smartphone aesthetics and functionality. This chapter delves into the subtle characteristics that contribute to the series' undeniable appeal, concentrating on the Titanium Frame of the Galaxy S24 Ultra, the streamlined one-mass design of the S24 and S24+, and the creative color selections inspired by earth minerals.

Introducing the Titanium Frame for the Galaxy S24 Ultra

The excellent Titanium Frame is at the heart of the Galaxy S24 Ultra's design, representing strength, durability, and high quality. Samsung has made a big step by putting titanium, a metal known for its strength and lightness, inside the smartphone's frame. This solution not only improves the device's structural integrity, but it also adds a degree of complexity that is consistent with the Galaxy S24 Ultra's premium positioning.

Titanium, recognized for its corrosion resistance and high tensile strength, maintains the Galaxy S24 Ultra's durability while retaining a sleek and slim appearance. The use of titanium goes beyond utility; it represents Samsung's dedication to enhancing the user experience by providing a device that not only performs well but also oozes elegance.

Furthermore, the titanium frame adds to the smartphone's general weight distribution, making it easier to grip and use. Samsung's rigorous engineering ensures that the titanium frame serves as both a functional component and a design statement, distinguishing the Galaxy S24 Ultra in a market dominated by traditional materials.

Streamlined One-Mass Design for S24 and S24 Plus

While the Galaxy S24 Ultra features a titanium frame, the S24 and S24+ have a sleek one-mass design that promotes seamless integration and ergonomic comfort.

Samsung's dedication to perfection is obvious in the same design language used across the Galaxy S24 Series.

The one-mass design avoids superfluous protrusions and assures a smooth transition from display to rear cover, resulting in a device that feels like an extension of the user's palm.

The S24 and S24+'s unibody structure adds to both its visual appeal and general longevity. The absence of visible seams or joints improves structural strength, resulting in a smartphone that not only looks great but also withstands the rigors of daily usage.

Furthermore, the simplified design allows for a more immersive visual experience. Reduced bezels and inconspicuous parts provide a broader canvas for the bright screens, letting users to watch content without interruptions. Samsung's devotion to a one-mass design demonstrates its attention to user-centric design concepts, in which form and function blend effortlessly.

Earth Mineral-Inspired Color Tones

In a departure from traditional smartphone color schemes, the Galaxy S24 Series features a palette inspired by earth minerals, giving the smartphones a sense of natural beauty. Samsung has deliberately designed a color palette inspired by the rich and diverse hues found in minerals, infusing the devices with elegance and distinctiveness.

The available colors vary from rich, glossy blues evocative of sapphires to warm, earthy tones reminiscent of copper and amber. Each hue symbolizes not just aesthetic appeal but also a link to the natural world, in line with current trends that stress sustainability and environmentally conscientious decisions.

The mineral-inspired color tones go beyond surface aesthetics, into the fundamental soul of the gadgets and producing an extraordinary visual experience.
The Galaxy S24 Series, with its earthy color palette, exemplifies Samsung's dedication to both technological and design innovation.

Additional online-only color options

In response to users' different tastes, Samsung provides new online-only color options for the Galaxy S24 Series. Recognizing the ever-changing nature of the digital world, these customized color variations appeal to those looking for a more personalized and unique smartphone experience.

These online-only color possibilities exceed the limitations of standard retail availability, allowing consumers to explore a broader range of alternatives. Whether it's a bold and colorful hue that makes a statement or a delicate, subdued tone that radiates refinement, Samsung's online-only selections allow consumers to express their own style.

The availability of unique colors online is consistent with Samsung's commitment to flexibility and customisation. In a world where personalization is key, these new color options allow customers to create a smartphone that not only satisfies their technology demands but also reflects their own style.

To summarize, the Galaxy S24 Series epitomizes precision technology and elegance in every detail. Samsung's painstaking dedication to design establishes a new benchmark for premium smartphones, from the Titanium Frame of the S24 Ultra to the streamlined one-mass design of the S24 and S24+, as well as the earth mineral-inspired color tones and extra online-only options. The Galaxy S24 Series is more than a collection of gadgets; it demonstrates Samsung's unrelenting dedication to innovation, user experience, and the pursuit of excellence in the world of mobile technology.

Product Specification

The Galaxy S24 Series is a technical wonder, combining cutting-edge innovation and exquisite attention to detail. This chapter looks into the detailed product specs for each model in the series: the Galaxy S24 Ultra, S24, and S24 Plus. From the display and size to camera capabilities, memory settings, battery specifications, and networking choices, every part of these devices has been meticulously designed to provide a really remarkable user experience.

Detailed Specifications for the Galaxy S24 Ultra, S24, and S24+

Display: The display is the window to the digital world, and Samsung has gone to great lengths to ensure that the Galaxy S24 Series offers an engaging and visually appealing experience.

- **Galaxy S24 Ultra:** The S24 Ultra has a 6.8-inch Dynamic AMOLED 2X display with a resolution of 3200 x 1440 pixels, which produces clear graphics and bright colors.

The HDR10+ support improves contrast and dynamic range, creating a visual feast for consumers.

- **<u>Galaxy S24 and S24+:</u>** These versions have slightly smaller screens (6.5 inches) but retain the amazing quality of Dynamic AMOLED 2X technology. The resolution is outstanding, at 2400 x 1080 pixels, assuring sharpness and clarity in all details.

<u>Dimensions and weight:</u>

The Galaxy S24 Series' design stresses sleekness while maintaining practicality.

- The Galaxy S24 Ultra has dimensions of 164.5 x 76.5 x 8.9mm and a weight of 215g.

- The Galaxy S24 has dimensions of 159.9 x 73.7 x 8.7mm and weighs 201g.

- Galaxy S24+ dimensions are 161.5 x 75.6 x 8.4mm, with a weight of 206 grams.

These proportions provide a perfect mix between a large display and a comfortable form factor, allowing customers to experience a big screen without losing mobility.

Camera:

The camera technology of the Galaxy S24 Series demonstrates Samsung's dedication to photographic quality.

- **Galaxy S24 Ultra:** A complex quad-camera configuration that includes a 108MP wide lens, a 48MP periscope telephoto lens, a 12MP ultrawide lens, and a 2MP depth sensor. This powerful camera system delivers remarkable definition, sharpness, and adaptability.

- **Galaxy S24 and S24+:** These versions include a triple-camera array that includes a 64MP wide lens, a 12MP ultrawide lens, and an 8MP telephoto lens. This arrangement provides a compromise between performance and efficiency, meeting a wide range of photographic requirements.

Memory and storage:

In the age of data-intensive apps and multimedia content, having enough memory and storage space is critical.

- **Galaxy S24 Ultra:** 8GB or 12GB of RAM, with internal storage options of 256GB, 512GB, or 1TB. The microSD card slot enables future expansion, meeting the demands of power users.

- **Galaxy S24 and S24+:** Users have the option of 6GB or 8GB of RAM, as well as 128GB or 256GB of internal storage. The microSD card slot offers versatility for individuals who need more capacity.

Battery:

Battery life is an important factor for contemporary smartphones, and the Galaxy S24 Series handles it with ample battery reserves.

- **Galaxy S24 Ultra:** A powerful 5,000mAh battery provides extended use, aided by features such as Adaptive Power Saving and Super Fast Charging.

- **Galaxy S24 and S24+:** These versions come with a 4,500mAh battery that is designed for efficiency and longevity. Super Fast Charging features are also available, allowing users to spend less time attached to charging wires.

Charging:

Samsung continues to push the frontiers of charging technology to provide consumers with ease and speed.

- **Galaxy S24 Ultra, S24, and S24+:** All models enable Super Fast Charging 2.0, which allows for a quick and efficient charging experience. Furthermore, Wireless PowerShare allows users to share their device's battery power with other compatible devices, increasing charging options.

Operating system (OS):

The Galaxy S24 Series operates on the most recent version of Samsung's user-friendly and feature-rich One UI, which is based on the Android platform.

Samsung Galaxy S24 Ultra, S24, and S24 Plus: One UI 7.0, which is based on Android 13, provides a seamless and intuitive user experience with frequent updates and security fixes.

Network & Connectivity:

In a world of hyper-networking, the Galaxy S24 Series offers a wide range of connectivity possibilities.

- **Galaxy S24 Ultra, S24, and S24+:** 5G compatibility means faster data rates and lower latency, ushering in a new age of connection. Bluetooth 5.2, NFC, and USB Type-C expand the connectivity possibilities, appealing to a wide range of user preferences and needs.

Finally, the Galaxy S24 Series product specs demonstrate Samsung's dedication to provide a complete and high-quality smartphone experience. From breathtaking screens to powerful camera systems, abundant memory and storage configurations, long-lasting batteries, and cutting-edge networking choices, these devices are precisely designed to fulfill the different demands of consumers in today's digital world. The Galaxy S24 Series is more than simply a collection of smartphones; it represents Samsung's commitment to pushing the limits of what is possible in the world of mobile technology.

A Comprehensive Look at Samsung's Advantages Over iPhones

In the ever-changing smartphone market, competition between Samsung's Galaxy series and Apple's iPhones has been at the forefront. Both companies have devoted followings and provide cutting-edge technology, but a closer look uncovers a slew of benefits that distinguish Samsung. Samsung has carved itself a separate market niche with its customizable possibilities, innovative features, and broad product offers.

Let's look at the entire benefits that Samsung has over iPhones.

1. **Different Product Range:** Samsung provides a diverse selection of smartphones that appeal to a variety of pricing ranges and customer preferences. From blockbuster handsets like the Galaxy S series to the more affordable Galaxy A series, Samsung has something for everyone. This

variety enables people to select a phone that meets their demands without sacrificing quality.

2. **Customization Options**: One of the most notable advantages of Samsung devices is the degree of customisation available. Android, Samsung's operating system, allows customers to fully customize their devices. Samsung customers have greater control over the appearance and feel of their cellphones than iPhone users do, with options ranging from changing themes and icon packs to creating custom widgets.

3. **Expandable Storage:** Samsung smartphones frequently provide expandable storage options, allowing users to quickly enhance their device's storage capacity with microSD cards. This functionality is especially useful for customers who want to save a big quantity of information, such as images, movies, and music, without having to rely entirely on cloud-based solutions.

4. **Innovative Display Technologies**: Samsung has been a pioneer in display technology, producing innovations such

as Super AMOLED, Infinity Displays, and fast refresh rates. These developments lead to brilliant colors, strong contrasts, and immersive viewing experiences. While iPhones have fantastic screens, Samsung's dedication to pushing the frontiers of display technology is clear in the spectacular images on their smartphones.

5. **Versatile Camera Systems:** The camera systems in Samsung smartphones, particularly flagship models such as the Galaxy S series, are well-known for their versatility and performance. With various lenses, high megapixel counts, and innovative features, Samsung handsets excel at capturing a wide range of shooting conditions. Furthermore, Samsung frequently includes cutting-edge camera technology such as periscope zoom lenses and superior image processing, allowing users to express their creativity in photography and filming.

6. **Innovative Features:** Samsung continually delivers novel features that improve the entire user experience. Samsung smartphones frequently have distinguishing features like as multitasking with split-screen views and S

Pen capability in some models. Samsung DeX, which transforms the smartphone into a desktop-like experience, exemplifies the company's dedication to pushing the limits of what a smartphone can do.

7. **Inclusion of the Headphone Jack**: While many smartphone manufacturers, including Apple, have discontinued the headphone jack, Samsung still includes it in several of their products. This move appeals to consumers who prefer conventional wired headphones, as it eliminates the need for dongles or other peripherals.

8. **Multi-Window Functionality:** Samsung's multi-window technology enables users to run numerous programs on the screen at the same time, improving multitasking capabilities. This functionality is very handy for productivity-driven individuals who wish to transition between programs without compromising efficiency.

9. **Price Versatility:** Samsung's product line includes devices at a variety of price points, giving users additional alternatives depending on their budget. This adaptability

enables customers to have access to cutting-edge technology and features without having to purchase flagship models, making Samsung smartphones more affordable to a wider range of consumers.

10. **<u>Durability and Build Quality:</u>** Samsung's products are well-known for their endurance and build quality. Premium materials and sturdy manufacturing processes ensure that Samsung smartphones can survive the rigors of regular use. Samsung stresses device lifespan and dependability, with features like as Corning Gorilla Glass protection and water and dust resistance.

11. **<u>Integration with Other Devices:</u>** Samsung's ecosystem goes beyond smartphones to include smartwatches, tablets, and other smart gadgets. The seamless integration of various gadgets results in a coherent environment, allowing consumers to have a synchronized and linked experience. This synergy is visible in features such as Samsung Flow, which allows for smooth device transitions and file sharing.

12. **<u>Broader App Store Options:</u>** While the Apple App Store is known for its tough app approval procedure, the Google Play Store for Samsung devices takes a more relaxed approach, allowing for a broader selection of applications. This freedom might be beneficial for consumers who want a variety of software selections but are not restricted by rigid app store regulations.

To summarize, Samsung has several benefits over iPhones, ranging from the freedom of the Android operating system to new features, diversified product selections, and user-friendly customization possibilities.

While iPhones have their advantages, Samsung's dedication to creating a diverse and personalized user experience has cemented its position as a leader in the competitive smartphone industry.

The continued battle between these two digital products continues to fuel innovation, providing customers with a steady supply of innovative technology and services.

Conclusion: A Culmination of Excellence in the Samsung Galaxy S24 Series

As we enter the last phase of our journey through the Samsung Galaxy S24 Series, it's time to synthesize the numerous features, innovations, and breakthroughs mentioned throughout this tour. The S24 Series is more than just a collection of smartphones; it combines cutting-edge technology, exquisite design, and user-centric features. Let us highlight the essential features and innovations that distinguish the Samsung Galaxy S24 Series, followed by some last views on its overall influence and relevance in the world of smartphones.

A summary of key features and innovations:

Design Elegance and Durability:

The Galaxy S24 Series exemplifies Samsung's dedication to precision technology and beauty in all aspects. The titanium frame, streamlined one-mass design for S24 and S24+, and earth mineral-inspired color tones all help to create a refined and visually attractive style. The inclusion of color options available exclusively online improves the level of customisation.

The ProVisual Engine Unleashes Creativity:

The ProVisual Engine includes groundbreaking technologies such as the Quad Tele System with greater zoom capabilities, Nightography for better low-light shooting, and AI editing tools like Erase, Re-compose, and Remaster. The Edit Suggestion and Generative Edit capabilities, together with Super HDR for lifelike previews, take the photography and filmmaking experience to new heights.

The Galaxy's Most Intelligent Experience Ever:

The Samsung Galaxy S24 Series is powered by the Snapdragon 8 Gen 3 Mobile Platform, which provides improved performance and efficiency. Adaptive refresh rates, gaming capabilities with ray tracing, bright displays with Vision Booster technology, and Corning Gorilla Armor for durability all contribute to an exceptional and intelligent user experience.

Revolutionizing Online Search:

The Circle to Search with Google and gesture-driven search functions transform user interactions with their devices. Generative AI-powered overviews for specific queries, location-based search upgrades, and the overall influence on information discovery represent a huge step forward in the world of online search.

Empowering Everyday Experiences:

Galaxy AI Features The overview includes Live Translate for barrier-free communication, Interpreter for real-time conversation transcription, Chat Assist for refining conversational tones, Android Auto connection for secure in-car communication, and Note Assist and Transcript Assist for better organization. These features help users with their regular interactions and communication.

Increased Security and Privacy:

Samsung Knox takes center stage in terms of security, offering consumers sophisticated intelligence settings, Knox Matrix, passkeys, increased data protection, and a seven-year update guarantee. The robust security mechanisms ensure that user data is safeguarded while privacy is respected.

The Next Step in Samsung's Environmental Journey:

Samsung's commitment to sustainability is demonstrated by the use of recycled materials in the Galaxy S24 Series, the incorporation of recycled cobalt and rare earth elements, the commitment to longer product lifecycles, UL ECOLOGO certification, carbon footprint verification, and the establishment of environmental goals for 2025. The series symbolizes an advancement in responsible and environmentally conscientious smartphone production.

Precision Technology and Elegance in Each Detail:

Samsung stresses precision technology and elegance in every aspect, from the titanium frame on the Galaxy S24 Ultra to the streamlined one-mass design on the S24 and S24+, as well as the earth mineral-inspired color tones.
The online-only color selections add to the device's status as a piece of sophisticated artistry rather than a mere utility.

Product Specification:

The Galaxy S24 Ultra, S24, and S24+ specifications cover a wide range of topics, including display, dimensions, weight, camera capabilities, memory configurations, storage options, battery specifications, charging capabilities, operating system information, and network and connectivity features. The specs emphasize the S24 Series' technical capabilities.

Final Thoughts on the Samsung Galaxy S24 Series:

The Samsung Galaxy S24 Series is more than just a line of smartphones; it demonstrates Samsung's constant commitment to innovation, user experience, and environmental responsibility. The series symbolizes a harmonic marriage of cutting-edge technology and design aesthetics, resulting in a gadget that goes beyond ordinary usefulness and becomes a companion in the user's journey.

As we say goodbye to this thorough guide, it's important to acknowledge the Samsung Galaxy S24 Series' effect on the smartphone landscape. The series pushes the frontiers of what a smartphone can do, whether through the ProVisual

Engine's creative powers, the intelligent features that fuel daily experiences, or the device's comprehensive security and privacy protections.

In an era where smartphones have become a vital part of our everyday lives, the Samsung Galaxy S24 Series emerges as a trailblazer, providing not just a product but also an experience. The series represents the pinnacle of advances in camera technology, display innovation, and sustainable production techniques, positioning it as a flagship not only for Samsung but for the whole industry.

In conclusion, the Samsung Galaxy S24 Series represents accuracy, creativity, and environmental conscience.
It encourages people to explore the boundless possibilities that technology may provide while upholding a commitment to sustainability. As consumers engage on their adventure with the Galaxy S24 Series, they enter a world where every detail is meticulously made, every feature is intended to empower, and every innovation exemplifies Samsung's unwavering quest of greatness.